WORSHIP and SOCIETY

E. K. Lee

M. A., M. Litt.

Canon Emeritus of Ripon Cathedral
and Chaplain of S. John's, Ripon

The Church Literature Association
Faith House 7 Tufton Street London SW1P 3QN
1977

First published January 1977
The Church Literature Association
Faith House 7 Tufton Street London SW1P 3QN

© 1976, E. KENNETH LEE

By the same author

The Religious Thought of St. John
The Meaning of Salvation
A Study in Romans

ISBN 0 85191 092 0

PREFACE

THE Archbishops have recently challenged the nation to consider what sort of society we are to aim at and what kind of people we must be to achieve that society. Many groups have been organized to discuss these matters. The danger is that these discussions should be regarded as something apart from the main stream of the Church's work, and that the response should be evaporated into a cloud of words.

One way in which these discussions could be more deeply impressed on the minds of people and given spiritual power is to draw them into the very heart of Christian worship. It is therefore argued in this booklet that worship, and especially the Eucharist, implies principles whereby all human institutions and systems are to be judged. If we can see that there is a close relationship between worship, the use of natural resources, and the kind of society we want, the work of social reform will take on a deeper dimension and be seen to be part of the will of God.

Worship itself will become richer and more meaningful. There is often too sharp a distinction made between worship and the affairs of the world and this is leading many people to abandon worship as irrelevant and out of date. The secularization of society is increasing and this for many people implies the widening of the gap between the Church and the world. It all depends on what we mean by "secularization". It may mean nothing more than the liberation of mankind from the grip of obscurantism; this is what Bonhoeffer meant by saying that man had "come of age". In this case the "secular man" may well be a human being who has assumed full responsibility for his life. He is not necessarily anti-religious and the Church would be wise to take a more positive view of secularization instead of attacking it as a threat to the Gospel.

Both worship and secularization (in the sense we have defined it) need each other; together they make an important contribution to the wholeness of life. The sacred and the secular are two aspects of one and the same thing, and either is incomplete and even wrong the moment that either wants to have a separated independent existence of its own. The universe is a whole and there is an internal relationship between all and every part of reality. If any part becomes isolated then it is like a cancer in the whole organism; it neither promotes life nor is it of any use to the affected part. Only worship can prevent secularization from becoming inhuman, and only secularization can save worship from being meaningless.

A number of suggestions for discussion have been added to the end of each chapter in order to stimulate, if need be, discussion in groups.

E. K. L.

CONTENTS

Chapter 1

THE RELATION OF WORSHIP TO CREATION

The basis of worship in the material universe is the immanence of God in his creation; for beneath the physical universe, as its animating source, lies the Eternal Logos, expressing and responding to the Eternal Father. Worship which is the response of creation to its Creator, therefore expresses the true relation of nature and man to the Creator. The unity of man with creation in the worship of God is found in Psalm 104, verses 20-24:

> Thou makest darkness, and it is night,
> When all the beasts of the forest creep forth.
> The young lions roar for their prey,
> Seeking their food from God.
> When the sun rises, they get them away
> and lie down in their dens.
> Man goes forth to his work
> And to his labour until the evening.
> O Lord how manifold are thy works!
> In wisdom hast thou made them all;
> The earth is full of thy riches.

We shall never discover the riches of worship if we do not include the whole of creation. The early Church was profoundly interested in nature. John of Damascus, for example, in his Easter hymns thinks that the Resurrection of Christ influenced not only man but physical creation too. S. Francis of Assisi implies that our attitude to men cannot be separated from our attitude to God's creatures. But in late medieval times and in the time of the Reformation there was an unfortunate pre-occupation with grace to the disadvantage of the works of nature. The tradition of the early church is preserved in some Eastern Liturgies. Here is a passage from an Eastern Liturgy which links the worship of man with the praises of nature:

> It is verily meet and right, fitting and due,
> to praise thee and bless thee,
> to worship thee, to glorify thee, to give thanks to thee,
> who madest all creation, visible and invisible,
> the fountain of life and immortality,
> the God and maker of all things;
> Whom heaven and the heaven of heavens hymn,
> And all their powers,
> the sun and moon, and all the choir of the stars,
> the earth, the sea, and all that is in them.

The words of the *Benedicite* and Harvest Festivals also keep alive the belief that material things belong to God and should be used by man to express praise and thanksgiving. Today, owing to the interest in conservation and the ravages of pollution, the intrinsic value of natural things is being realised. Although the Christian attitude to nature has been condemned in a recent essay by Lynn White (in *Science*, vol. 155, pp 1203ff), we believe that the invisible God is seen through the visible things of creation that he has made. There are scientists who tell us that within the animal creation the appreciation of beauty, the sense of order, and the dawning of a moral sense, can be observed. These elements only come to full consciousness in man, but there is a unity and cohesion between man and nature with which few theologians have yet come to terms. The concept of God being at work within the processes of life and nature, rather than by acting upon them from the outside, as it were, radically affects our understanding of worship. Worship is not something to do with only the heart and soul of man, but involves all creation. Just as we are urged to enlarge our conception of God, so too must we widen our understanding of worship to include the material world. The words of the *Benedicite* in Morning Prayer will then take on a new significance and reality and we shall realize the full implications of using bread and wine in the chief act of Christian worship.

Worship in human experience arises from the reaction of the spiritual consciousness in man to the mystery of life, and to some aspects of his physical environment. It is man's spirit reaching out to something or someone greater than himself, as the source of all being and the power that fills and sustains it. At all times and in all places there have been those who are sensitive to the immediate encounter with the infinite and who respond to it with cosmic emotions, and who at such moments pass beyond the realms of time and space. There are indeed those who experience such 'awe' in the presence of the mysterious and beautiful without any theistic implications, but there are others who pass beyond the vague feeling of the 'numinous' to the worship of the Holy God who illuminates and elucidates the whole of their experience of reality.

Worship in its widest sense is the reaction of every part of creation to this power whom we call God. Its quality and value for man is proportionate to the truth and sublimity of his idea of God, and to the sincerity of his response, which is integral to his existence as a human being. It may be only a superstitious response or it may be the rational and concious worship of God as revealed in the life and teaching of Jesus Christ.

From the first almost every form of worship has included sacrifice. It is found right through the Old Testament, for example, from the story of Cain and Abel in Genesis chapter four to the prophecy of Malachi: 'In every place incense shall be offered unto my name, and a pure offering.' In the minds of many people the sole form of sacrifice was the taking of life and the only purpose was the expiation of sin. But the meaning and form of sacrifice was much wider than that. According to the Old Testament the purpose of sacrifice was first of all *life* through the sharing of blood in communion, then the giving of gifts and making of homage, the rendering of first fruits, the giving of thanks. All these things play a much larger part than expiation in the universal purposes of sacrifice. The forms of sacrifice, too, were varied; there was the slaying which symbolized the surrender of life, but there was also the ritual offering of things, corn, wine, oil, gold and silver; the spiritual sacrifice of penitence, prayer and righteousness.

The connection of the rich complex and meaning of sacrifice with God's creation is obvious. We praise God for his making of things by taking things and offering them to him in acknowledgement of our awareness of his goodness. We take bread and wine and offer these to God exactly as the Jew of old, and beyond him the primitive peoples dimly feeling after God, the creator of all things. Indirectly the sacredness of all things is recognized by the use we make of them in worship.

There is thus an organic unity between man and the natural creation from which he cannot extricate himself. Man has arisen out of the natural world and continues to be part of it. The laws of nature and the moral law are both manifestations of the Creator; there is a givenness in both for they are both rooted in the Being of God who is the source of all things. But man has left behind a passive conformity to the laws of nature such as is characteristic of the rest of creation. He has a sense of responsibility which includes the material creation of which he is a part but which is ever widening so that it covers all the activities of man. Just as the Christian has the responsibility for living his life according to the purpose of God either as a private individual or in society, so too has he the responsibility of using the natural creation in such a way that it will bring forth its potentialities in harmony with God's purposes. He is more likely to be aware of this responsiblity if it is explicit in his acts of worship.

In thus emphasizing the close relation of worship to the natural creation, it must be Nature as understood by the Christian. Our understanding of man's setting in the world must be seen in the light of the Redemption achieved by Christ. God is worth nothing less than the homage of the whole creation. Yet creation is diverted by sin from its proper end, namely, God's glory; it has become divided against itself. Man recapitulates in himself the whole of creation, the inanimate and animal life that preceded him in order of time; he is the crown of a long course of evolution.   He does not isolate himself from what has gone before towards the making of him nor is there any reason to suppose that the development has come to an end. It was through man's greatness that the rebellion against God began; only man can *sin* for only man has moral choice. This has affected for ill the material environment in which he lives. Evil which had its origin in the sinful will of man has become so embedded in society and the environment that it seems to acquire a life of its own in the material universe. In this sense the natural world is in need of redemption. Only man could achieve this, for only he is free and only he epitomizes in himself the whole creation. With astonishing insight Paul expressed the cosmic redemptive work of Jesus in the following words: 'For it pleased the Father that in him should all fullness dwell; and having made peace through the blood of the cross, by him to reconcile all things unto himself; by him, I say, whether they be things in earth, or things in heaven' (Col. 1. 19, 20), or again, 'that in the dispensation of the fullness of times he might gather together in one (recapitulate) all things in Christ, both which are in heaven, and which are on earth' (Eph. 1.10). In the redemption achieved by Christ we see the ideal of all creation turning to God in perfect worship, nature redeemed from perversion by sin to perfection in Christ. Man is redeemed so that the whole creation might worship God worthily. Such worship is dependent on the reconciliation effected by the redemptive act of the Son of God, a reconciliation which involves the whole creation brought into union with Christ.

In Christian worship, therefore, the moral consciousness should be stimulated by the sense of the 'numinous' — of 'awe' in God's presence. The realization of God's presence, moreover, should be accompanied by an understanding of God's purposes for man and the world; and man's response should be expressed in sacrifice, the offering of one's self and the things of this world in the service of God, in active co-operation with God's purpose in the world. The point at which the sense of the 'numinous' and the awareness of social responsibility meet in man's consciousness is in the realization of his place and the world's place in God's purpose.

This is foreshadowed in the Old Testament conception of 'righteousness.' God himself was regarded as 'Righteousness;' in fact righteousness was not merely a moral principle, but a numinous quality — it produced awe and reverence in the minds of men. It was something bigger and more fundamental than morality. Our Lord enlarged this idea of righteousness until it was seen to be identified with Divine love. In Romans 1.17 righteousness is regarded as being inherent in God and imparted to man. This Divine righteousness is revealed in the life of individuals and in the movements of the world and of society.

Inspite of this union of the numinous and the ethical, there is a real danger lest Christians should endeavour to build up their religious life either upon devout feelings or upon the performance of moral duties. This separation is destructive of the wholeness of the Christian life and experience. True worship is vitally related to the response made by the Logos to the Eternal Father manifest throughout the whole creation, and therefore can never involve a withdrawal of interest from the visible order, or an attempt to satisfy devotional instincts apart from the acceptance of ethical responsibility within the created order. On the other hand, concentration upon the moral claims of Christianity is by itself inadequate of our understanding of worship. It is but a partial recognition of the facts about Jesus. His ethical teaching cannot be divorced from our understanding of his person. He himself claims that the acceptance or rejection of his message is the acceptance or rejection of the immanence of God and that faith in God is not possible without a confession of faith in him, in his teaching and person. Furthermore, his earthly ministry culminated in the mighty acts of the Resurrection and Ascension. It is only when we realize that in our worship we are united with the risen, ascended and glorified Saviour that we can know the real significance of his teaching and receive the power necessary to obey him.

We need therefore to combine in our Christian life the study of our Lord's teaching as expressed in the New Testament and interpreted in the history of the Church with the practice of worship through which his presence is made real to us and we are made aware of our responsibility for the right use of material things and our fellowship one with another. In this way the moral teaching and challenge of our Lord, both to the individual person and to society, are made effective by the grace of the same ever-present Lord.

Our Lord himself exhibited the perfect combination and interaction of the devotional and practical elements of religion. He regularly attended public worship at the local synagogues and in the Temple at Jerusalem. He spent long periods in prayer. On the other hand, he went about doing good, performing all kinds of practical service. Many of his parables deal with the practical duties of men and women. His teaching about prayer showed that people should find help and strength in the presence of God. The acts of God in the Incarnation, the Cross and Resurrection, disclose the same truths: that in Christ there is revealed a 'numinous' quality along side a perfect human response by obedience to the moral law of service and self-oblation.

The essence of worship is that it enables us to see the vision of God. In the light of that vision we see all things transfigured — the world as it was meant to be and will yet be made. We see, too, that in and through Jesus Christ we have a share in realizing that vision upon earth. We are transported with joy and pour out ourselves in adoration, just as we do on a much lower scale when a glorious view of nature comes into sight. Thus inspired we go out into the world of commerce, into the lives of ordinary men and women, determined to express that vision in life and to make all life an act of worship because all life is intended to be a response to the vision of God.

Public worship is the corporate ascription to God of his true worth and the placing of ourselves as creatures in our true relationship to him as Creator and so to the rest of creation. This follows from the recognition that we and all creation are dependent on God's continuous creative activity, and are meant to glorify him as Creator and to fulfil his purposes. That is to say, creation and the whole of life is sacramental and exists for the glory of God.

In view of the fact that fellowship between man and God is constantly being disrupted by sin, the relations between men marked by violence and division, and the material things of God's universe abused and exploited, the Christian community will constantly recall to mind the redemption wrought by Christ. This in itself will stir our hearts with gratitude. 'We bless thee for our creation, preservation, and all the blessing of this life; but above all, for thine inestimable love in the redemption of the world by our Lord Jesus Christ.' Only by his redemption are we brought into the position in which the creature can truly worship the Creator. But in addition to the confession of human sin and the acceptance of pardon as necessary elements in worship, the Christian community will be deeply conscious of its own special need of penitence and grace, both for forgiveness and for more efficient service. Only on the basis of confessing its own specific sins of disunion and faithlessness, and its conformity to the world's standards, and by accepting the divine forgiveness and help can it offer itself, its soul and body, to the Father in Christ, to work for him for the fulfilment of his purposes for mankind.

In all the services of the Church, the fundamental meaning of worship which we have indicated, is involved. There can indeed be no true act of worship in which it is not implied. In the response we make in Morning and Evening Prayer, we should be consciously relating the whole of life to its divine end. Indeed, the validity of every private act of worship depends on the same underlying principle. It is partly for this reason that the reading of the Bible is so valuable an accompaniment of worship, for its emphasis upon God's creatorship, upon his moral lordship, and upon his redemptive action within history, is a constant reminder of the fact that our relation with God involves all our relations with men and things. But it is in the Eucharist that the central and most profound interpretation of the meaning of worship is experienced.

In every act of worship because we are incarnate in physical bodies and dwell in a material environment, we must necessarily make use of material things. The most absorbed prayer and meditation involves the action of the brain, which is related to the body and thus to the whole creation. The Eucharist, in the emphasis which it places upon bread and wine, calls attention in a very emphatic manner to the material world, and to its relation with man's spiritual destiny. The very fact that bread and wine are said to become for the faithful the Body and Blood of Christ, indicates in the first place the essential view of the nature and function of the material world. The Christian believes that the material world exists to be God's means of communicating with his children. Material things are the means by which man grows into perfect fellowship with and likeness to the Father. 'All things are in their measure an expression of the Will which sustains and also moulds and guides all things, so that the unity of the world, its principle of rational coherence, is the Divine Personality in self-expression' (William Temple).

Obviously if material things are so closely related to the Creative Word that they may be regarded in *any* sense as expressing his will and presence, there can be no final dualism in the universe. Matter is not independent of God, nor is it, in itself, intractable to his purposes. It is of divine origin, and may serve on its own level as the means of communication between God and man. There is a great deal of truth in Whitman's lines:

Strange and hard the paradox here I give,
Objects gross and unseen are one.

It is very significant, therefore, that in the Christian worship, material things are regarded as becoming the instrument of God's purpose, under certain well defined conditions. This achievement is confined in the Eucharist to a fragmentary selection of the material world. Bread and wine, set within the community of the faithful, assembled for the purpose, are offered with particular intention, and become the expression of Christ's presence and union with his people. Yet, inspite of this limitation, the meaning of the Eucharist in Christian life and thought would be obscured unless it is seen that the Eucharistic relation of the Christian community to the material elements is intended to be prophetic and representative of the true relation of men to the whole created order.

The prophetic nature of the Eucharist is seen when we reflect that its bread and wine are drawn from the world of nature and are often exploited and abused by industry and commerce. Those elements are representative of the natural, social and economic order. In the act of consecration a prophetic judgement is passed upon a world in which bread and wine, and all they represent, are cornered by speculators and adulterated by manufacturers; a world in which the interests of money misrepresent God's bounty and create artificial poverty. The Eucharist takes the common means of bodily sustenance for which the world struggles and swindles, and restores them to their proper place as instruments of human fellowship. But it can do this only because it first restores them to their proper relation to God in Christ.

If God is the sole creator of all things, and if his creative act arises, not out of any imperfection or deficiency in his Being, but from his infinite love, then all created things must be intended to serve the ends of love. This means that when within the created order the levels of consciousness and moral freedom appear, there will arise the possibility of the communion of the creature with the Creator. This is the supreme gift that Eternal Love can bestow upon the creature, and in accordance with this, Christian theology asserts that the true end of man is the Beatific Vision. No such capability is found in the sub-human creation; and this raises the question of the relation between man and the rest of the created order.

The nature of that relation is suggested by the structure of the world in which we can see several stages — matter, life, mind. We can see that matter is the instrument of life, and that matter and life together are instruments of mind. And in man, matter, life and mind are instruments of spirit. There is continuity in the progress and progress in the continuity. What emerges at each stage of development is dependent on what existed before, and raises the previous existence to a higher level, and gives it richer meaning. But if there is unity in this creative progress and if in the end there is communion between creature and Creator, and if man is the creature in which this possibility is to be fully realized, then he can exert his freedom aright only if he treats the material in harmony with this ultimate purpose and with the reverence due to so important a part of God's creation.

It is only through such an attitude of respect that the rest of the created order, with which he is organically related, can rise to its full meaning and is capable of being, in the richest sense, and in its own right, the expression of divine purpose. This means that the created universe is full of sacramental possibility; but the realization of this depends on mankind — not that it is thought of as a mere human achievement; the whole possibility is given by God and awaits man's response. All this is implicit in the use made of bread and wine in the Church's central act of worship.

QUESTIONS on Chapter 1

1   Discuss the different objects of a man's worship. Is it a natural human instinct? Why has the worship of God declined in recent years?

2   Is there any relation between worship and conduct?

3   Should we banish 'the world' from our minds when worshipping God?

4   'Man is redeemed so that the whole Creation might worship God.' Discuss this statement.

5   In what ways is the sacramental idea of material things frustrated by modern society?

6   In what ways does the structure and witness of the Church compromise the truths for which it stands?

Chapter 2

THE RELATION OF WORSHIP TO REDEMPTION, OFFERING AND COMMUNION

No theology that is either adequate to truth or competant for dealing with life can neglect the fact of sin. It is generally asserted that sin breaks a man's fellowship with God and dislocates all human society. But it produces a further disaster — it involves a violent distortion of his relation with the material world. Nature, man and society are inter-related in the work of redemption. And the Eucharist not only proclaims the true relation which man has set aside, but proclaims also its restoration. This act of worship reassures the worshipper that material things, man and society are the objects of God's love and redemption.

While Christian thought has emphasized the truth that the physical world is the work of God, and is intended to serve him, it has not been very clear about the way in which the material order has been affected by sin. The ancient curse as set forth in Genesis 3.17-19 declares that in consequence of Adam's disobedience the earth will yield him a livelihood only at the price of toil and sweat. A further development of this thought is that man's sin has actually debased the natural world, in the sense that it has produced the savagery of wild beasts, and the catastrophes of plague, tempests and earthquakes.

The conception of evolution of man seems, if accepted, to falsify all such teaching. The knowledge available to us today about the origin of the earth does not allow us to establish a simple casual relation between man's sin and the existence of the numerous ills which afflict nature. These ills existed, at least in certain forms, before the appearance of man; they are still observable today in spheres where it is impossible to connect them with human sin. What is more, they are in many cases the necessary condition and natural basis, for the very life of the creative process.

Further reflection, however, shows that even if we accept the scientific idea of evolution, the doctrine of the effects of the Fall upon the natural order embodies a profound element of truth. While it is impossible to maintain that human sin has caused an actual change in the nature of the physical universe, nevertheless, the two conceptions of evolution and human freedom, taken together, enable us to see that the misuse of freedom exercised upon the natural environment, may well have the effect of retarding or distorting the development of the natural order.

In Romans 8.18-23, Paul writes of the entire creation sighing and throbbing waiting for the coming of the redeemed children of God. In some way the failure of man has frustrated nature from fulfilling the purposes for which God intended. And in one sense we can see how: if the natural order is to be the instrument whereby man attains his divinely appointed end, then, man's false and evil purposes must be held to degrade the order of nature, including his own body. Man uses the material world for selfish purposes and thus distorts its meaning. And even if it is to be said that there are evils in the natural order for which man cannot be held responsible — earthquakes, floods and terrible diseases — we may yet hold that man's sin and his selfish preoccupation have retarded such investigation as might have led to his mastery over them; and they have certainly caused his failure to practise the sympathy and self-sacrifice which such diseases ought to evoke. It is unquestionable that man's attempt to carry out the exploitation of natural resources, has created a vicious circle. A false order of life is set up, which reacts upon man himself, perverting his judgement, so that the task of doing what is right throws upon him unnatural moral strain, and distorts his whole moral life.

Because of the presence of evil in the world it is a reason for profound hope that Christian theology extends redemption beyond human beings to the whole of creation. It is a process which is even now at work as creation moves forward to the fulfilment of whatever God may have in mind for it. The ultimate goal of creation is a spiritual one so the process involves the ultimate transformation of matter. The so-called material is simply its lowest mode of expression. It is the foundation for subsequent stages which expand and realize its implicit powers and virtues. To assert that the world is the creation of an infinite God allows for endless possibilities of growth and improvement. God being thought, will and love, the world in which he is immanent must be open to redemption. This fact invests the smallest phenomena, material or other, with dignity and meaning. Each has its place in a spiritual whole, which will find its fruition in the 'manifestation of the sons of God,' those who have been redeemed by Christ. The Christian faith thus offers us a unifying picture of reality, man and nature together experiencing the fulfilment of God's purposes for his world. There is an intricate net-work that links together everything from the smallest inanimate object to the highest human achievement.

Even now we can see signs of the redemption of the body. Consider the case of a good man: his body has its place in his total experience; it declares its needs and imposes its conditions. But it is made to minister to the functions of reason, imagination, and moral sense. And thus it is that the spirit is ever asserting its inherent right to rule and guide. Matter is not abolished: it remains the basis, but it is taken up, transformed, redeemed, in the higher stages of the process. A picture by Raphael is but a further manifestation of the cosmic trend that evolves a rose; so is the transformation of a house into a home.

We can see, therefore, that the doctrine of the relation between human action and the natural order is not to be lightly dismissed. It is of the utmost importance for the Christian doctrine of society, for it leads to the conclusion that the full redemption of man must be effective in the whole organic relation in which he finds himself. Redeemed man must at least seek the right employment of natural means and resources — he must seek so to organise his action in the natural world as to bring his earthly pursuits into line with his heavenly destiny. Thus the natural will fulfil its true function as the minister of the spiritual.

This organic redemption is set forth in the Eucharist, where the Church as the redeemed society of men, exercising upon bread and wine the redeemed purpose, and devoting them in fellowship to the service of God, finds in those elements a means of divine communion. Here the natural order is brought back to its true function. But since the Eucharist proclaims the Gospel of Jesus Christ, and that Gospel is of universal scope, the Eucharist has a revolutionary meaning for the whole life of the world. This must be so, for the Eucharist is the central act of the Church; but the Church is the body of Christ, and its central, characteristic act is the act of Christ himself, risen, ascended and triumphing over the world of sin.

We shall see that the Eucharist is never merely an act of individual piety. The necessary human action in it always includes the action of the Church, the society redeemed by the Cross and Passion of Christ, though the Church requires in each communicant an intention consonant with its own purpose. This claim is based on the fact that through Baptism each member has been admitted into the society which is the Body of Christ. What is declared in the Eucharist is that redemption is intended to restore human personality, within a fellowship which shall include the whole of life, and shall employ the material environment as an instrument of the divine-human communion.

We have already remarked upon the central place which sacrifice occupies in religion. We now observe that it is found at the heart of Christian worship. The Eucharist is the proclamation of the 'full, perfect, and sufficient' sacrifice of Christ upon the Cross. The Biblical word 're-membrance' does not mean any sort of remembrance, but a recalling, a manifestation, in the present by word or deed. The word used by Paul and rendered in English as 'show,' comes from the same root as the word commonly translated 'gospel' and means 'declare,' 'proclaim,' or 'show forth.' When therefore the Church meets to celebrate the Eucharist it is for the recalling of Christ's act of redemption in the context of worship. By the Eucharistic act Christ's death and resurrection and ascension are 'proclaimed' till he come.

The Eucharist is a sacrifice in so far as it is the 'memorial' of Christ's sacrifice upon the Cross. It is a memorial of his sacrifice because the Church presents it to Father as a living and present intercession; it is the sacrament of Christ because it makes it present before the Church as an effective and actual means of reconciliation and communion. The Eucharist, as the memorial of the redemption won by Christ, is one with the Cross and with the heavenly intercession of Christ.

Having proclaimed the reconciliation won on the cross, the Church in the Eucharist commits the whole realm of the world's life to the same acceptance and deliverance. Here in its most sacred moment, Christian worship confronts the practical, economic, and political disorder in man's sinful world with a new order already sacramentally realized; and at this point worship reaches its widest and richest reality; for it is here that the real meaning of communion is revealed.

The Eucharist proclaims the reconciliation of man to God; the re-alignment of man and his world with the divine purpose; and it therefore throws emphasis upon the offering of self to God. And since Christian theology constantly maintains the value and meaning of the human person, the central act of Christian worship requires in each communicant a personal offering of himself. Unlike the secular and totalitarian systems of our time, the Redeemed Society does not demand the paralysis of the personal centres of life. It requires the co-operation of their voluntary self-surrender to God, in which their freedom is consecrated and enlarged. Each faithful communicant comes into communion with God, not that his free personality may be overwhelmed, but that he may become a worker together with God.

The Church does not repress the personal initiative of God's children; the Church is a true fellowship of man with God in which each individual has personal relations with his Creator and Redeemer. A man's value is not merely his value to himself, nor is it merely his value to society: a man's value is his value to God. Yet this communion is never individualistic. The act of Communion is performed within the Christian Fellowship, and is the mode of ever deepening integration with the community of believers. The growth of his personality is dependent upon the fellowship of the whole body. The fellowship is a condition of growth. When everything has been said about the personal value of the individual, it needs to be stressed that that value is starved apart from fellowship.

Thus there need be no contradiction between the self-offering of each individual and the corporate oblation of the Church. The personal and social is preserved, strengthened and unified as it is placed in harmony with the Divine will. And the completion of this unification is found in the offering to God of the common material instrument of the world, represented by bread and wine, which now becomes the sign and instrument of a communion more than human; of the integration of men with Christ, the Creative Word of God and Redeemer of men.

The offering of ourselves, our souls and bodies to God, in union with the eternal sacrifice of Christ, then, is at once corporate and personal. As individuals we unite ourselves to the Bread of Life, to the living, immanent and transcendent Christ, by making communion with him; but by so doing we are also brought into communion with our fellow-worshippers everywhere, and since the sacrifice of Christ was offered not for the favoured few, but for all people of all ages, Holy Communion brings us into a new relationship with his redemptive purpose for the whole human race. The words, 'Here we offer and present unto thee, O Lord, ourselves, our souls and bodies to be a reasonable, holy and lively sacrifice' were never meant to be an individual prayer, it is the offering up to God of the whole fellowship of the Church united as the Body of Christ in him.

The wider world is brought into that stream of offering through the intercessions. The Offertory and the Intercessions are inseparately involved in each other. If the bread and wine represent in a general way the world of business and commerce, the intercessions bring into our worship the particular needs of people, nations and industry. Intercessory prayer is not merely a message sent to God, telling him how he should behave in the world. It is part of the prayer and offering of the Great High Priest. It is the means by which those for whom we pray are carried into the self-offering of Christ and we are united with them in our desire to become instruments of God's purpose and channels through which he can act. It is therefore a costly operation: a prayer which is a mere request, without self-offering is not a prayer in Christ's Name. To bring the world before God is to be prepared to answer God's question, 'Whom shall I send and who will go for us?' This means that during the most devout parts of worship we are still in the world where men live and work. And where the Church fails in evangelistic and missionary effort, it falls short of the Eucharistic act.

In some places the Intercessions are made by a layman, reminding us that the Eucharist is most emphatically the people's affair. Liturgy and laity come from the same root; it is the whole Christian community that is loosed from sin by the blood of Christ and made by him priests unto his God and Father. Unless we dismiss the references in the New Testament to the priesthood of all believers as mere hyperbole, we are compelled to recognize the real share of the laity in the offering of the Eucharistic sacrifice.

This carries with it grave responsibilities. Because God is revealed in Christ as love, and supremely so on the Cross, sacrifice cannot be offered to him apart from service to, and love of, the men and women who are his children. It is not enough to say that worship means the good life. It is more true to say that the good life means worship. But the fact is that the two are inseparable except in thought. The life of service and self-sacrifice for mankind which is demanded of all who are involved in politics, economics, industry and education, is an integral part of what is offered to God in the course of Eucharistic worship.

Thus every Christian is pledged to uphold the standard of life expressed in the Eucharist in so many different ways. This will involve for each one a constant struggle against public opinion around him and the social order in which he lives, as he seeks to share in the building up of a Christian community in the place where he lives. The Archbishop of Canterbury has recently pin-pointed some of the evils which are destroying society and against which Christians must use the sword. Dirt on the media, far too high an abortion rate, cheapening of sex, lack of reverence for life, unemployment, bad houses, lack of playing fields. Fighting against these evils, he says, is not pleasant work, but if the Church is ready to do its work it must be ready 'to smite and smite again' if we are going to achieve the kind of society implied in our acts of worship.

The Christian is encouraged to do this because the Eucharist is not only the memorial of a sacrifice, it also shows forth the power of the Resurrection. That power is rightly considered as transforming and re-newing the personal lives of believers; but we need also to regard the Risen and Victorious Lord as indwelling his Church, so that the Church is seen and believed to be his Risen Body. It is this corporate association with the living Christ triumphing over death and defeating all the disin-tegrating forces of sin, that gives a unique note of confidence to the Church's worship. It is in this confidence that the Church finds courage to confront the world's hostility; and it is in union with its risen Lord that it finds its assurance that it will triumph in the end. The Eastern Church through its liturgy teaches that the whole creation will be trans-figured by the power of the Resurrection. This means that all the splendour of the natural world and the creative achievements of men have eternal significance; nothing will ultimately be lost.

One of the evidences of the presence of the Risen Lord in his Church will be seen in its ability to be flexible in its approach to the people of our day. Only that which is dead remains static and without the power of adaptation. It may be that to be faithful to the reality of the Gospel we must express it in radically different ways from those to which we have been accustomed. When we present the mysteries of the faith, we must be attentive to the cultural and sociological milieu in which the Word is proclaimed. But in our eargerness to be 'modern' we should remember that there is something permanent about the problems of existence, and that there are abiding truths in the Eucharistic act of worship which must not be obscured by thoughtless revision or a superficial understanding of the modern mind.

The members of the worshipping community should get together and discover for themselves what these abiding truths are and to consider ways and means of making the Church more effective as the Body of Christ in witnessing Christ's challenge to the world today. In time a congregation which began to feel its unity in this way, and became conscious of its responsibility for representing Christ in the world, would find itself impelled to speak as he spoke, to champion the cause of the weak and of the oppressed, to rebuke the exploiter and avaricious, and, perhaps as a consequence, to be hated by the world as he was hated. By ceasing to be merely pious and devout, the congregation would in this way become once again Christian. In the next chapter we shall consider what these fundamental truths are which we proclaim every time we take part in Eucharistic worship.

QUESTIONS on Chapter 2

1   Discuss the ways in which sin has affected the natural creation.

2   What bearing do you think Christ's cosmic redemption has upon our understanding of the creation?

3   Is the idea of offering in union with Christ's sacrifice made clear in recent revisions of the liturgy?

4   What is meant by 'the priesthood of the laity?' Should this be limited to ecclesiastical matters?

5   What permanent elements in Christian society should be reflected in the liturgy?

Chapter 3

THE SOCIAL IMPLICATIONS OF WORSHIP

Strictly speaking this chapter heading should read 'The Social Implications of Christian *theology*.' The truth is that both worship and sociology arise out of Christian doctrine, out of the teaching of the Christian Faith as to what man is and his relation to creation and to God. We are not to decide what sort of worship we would like and then try and square our sociology with it or, *vice-versa*, decide on our sociology and then try and square our worship with that. Both worship and sociology are dependent on the nature of man and the material world and their relations to one another and to God who created them. By his very essence, by the sort of being that he is, man is in organic relation to the rest of the human community and to the material world of which his body is a part. Out of this situation two main problems arise.

Man finds himself threatened with the Scylla and Charybdis of an individualism which denies the claims of society, and a collectivism which denies the claims of the person. The solution of this problem cannot be found, so long as human life is envisaged only upon a secular plane: it is only as he knows himself destined for the Kingdom of God that man can discover the unity of his personal and corporate life. The second social implication of Christian theology is concerned with man's approach to the resources of the material world for the satisfaction of his natural needs. It is only as the satisfaction of material needs is seen to be related to God's will that material goods will be sought in a manner which does not contradict man's true nature.

In Christian worship the true political life of man is declared to be, not necessarily a perpetual conflict, or even balance, of selfish opposed forces, but the mode of expressing in certain necessary human contacts the unity of the personal and corporate purposes of life. And man's economic activity is revealed in its proper purpose, not as a self-regarding scramble for temporal satisfaction, but as a necessary step towards the goal of divine-human communion. In worship we behold the essential political and economic characteristics of human nature directed to their proper end, brought into harmony with God's purposes for his creation.

It is clear that the situation that faces us is very far from the ideal envisaged in the previous paragraph. But the actual situation emphasises the relevance of the Eucharist as it constantly challenges the world in which we live. The peculiar sin which has overtaken Western man is consumer mentality, that is a mentality which finds the whole of life in getting, spending, having. Such an acquisitive mentality developes into an aggressive mentality, and this in its turn thinks nothing of exploiting both nature and human beings without a sense of responsibility. This attitude to life has acquired such a dominance in the modern world that men are apt to make it the sole interpretation of themselves and of life as a whole. In a world from which God has been banished it is difficult to find rational grounds for believing the sacredness of life. There can be no remedy for the present disorder in society unless the present absorption of interest in such limiting values and horizons can be broken. There must be an awareness of a larger interpretation of life that will make room for a transcendent Reality which permeates the whole of life. One pathway to this larger world of Reality is worship.

Worship helps to put social service into its right place, for we seek the reformation of society in such a way that it will not turn men from their true end in life. It is easy to picture a society in which juster distribution of wealth, more widely diffused culture, and international peace, which though diminishing external evils, may effect no redemption of human nature. A democratic order beneath which there is a religious vacuum is not likely to survive, much less generate the power to resist totalitarianism in one or other of its forms. William Temple never uttered a wiser word than when he said that 'the most effective thing the Church can do in the world, and the most effective thing any individual Christian can do, is to lift up his heart in adoration to God.' When we do this we enlarge our understanding of life in such a way that the conflicting interests can be transcendented.

The world needs to discover a powerful centre of unity if it is not going to destroy itself in mutual conflict and in the pursuit of widely contrasted aims. Man has reached a stage at which he can no longer afford to live under conditions which are analogous to those of England under the heptarchy. Economic interdependence and modern means of communication have a profound effect for good or ill upon the whole of life. We are called to be citizens of the world, and the need for human unity is such that without it mankind faces the prospect of destruction. We know, for example, that the gap between nations who are relatively wealthy and the nations that are relatively poor, unless active steps are taken to prevent it, will widen to a point at which there will be no option except to face world strife or an imposed domination. The world therefore needs to discover a common aim and purpose if it is going to survive.

But if there is one clear lesson of history it is that men do not live by bread alone. A united humanity that found its unity only on the basis of economic goods and material comfort would be what Plato called 'a city of pigs,' not a human society. All human societies need a purpose and an inspiration, and for Christians there can be no doubt that this unity must be found in Christ. It is a *religious* unity that the world needs. For this reason worship, as we have already suggested, is a powerful unifying force.

In this respect the Christian doctrine of the organic unity of man with his physical environment is of immense significance. Material things are important not only because of their functional utility but also because of the influence they have upon human nature. We develope relationships with things; things affect our sense of continuity and discontinuity. Our attitude to things and our experience of material conditions can radically affect our judgements about life and people. Yet through our abuse of the natural resources of the world we are busy destroying the world as a suitable place for human habitation. Pesticides and herbicides filter into our foods injuring our bodies. We risk the pollution of the oceans destroying immeasurable quantities of marine life. The answer to this is not less technology but more responsible technology. So worship in which bread and wine occupies the central place is supremely relevant to the present situation. In the Eucharist it is demonstrated that the industrial order symbolized by the bread and wine can be brought within the redeeming action of Christ. In the Eucharist the totality of the world is involved.

A form of worship in which the whole emphasis is placed on personal piety and individual salvation is a maimed version of Christ's religion. But a Christianity which is inspired to try and consecrate the whole of life so that it becomes, like the Eucharistic Bread, something in which Christ reigns can become a spiritual force transforming all life. 'The consecration of the eucharistic elements is matched by and interwoven with the consecration of the participants so that they too become through the sacrament the means whereby they fulfil God's purposes in the world' (Report, *Man and Nature*, p 60).

The Eucharist is clearly a sacrament of fellowship. Communion with the Lord of necessity involves communion with our fellow Christians. It is at the Eucharist that we share the one common table, and are nourished by the self-same food. Kneeling together at the Altar rails to receive the common Saviour of us all, the rich and poor, white and black, people of different wordly status, are reminded that in Christ they are one family, that with God there is no distinction either of wealth, colour or status.

Such fellowship exhibits an essential characteristic of human nature. It is sometimes said that industry ought to be co-operation for public service rather than competition for private gain. The essential purpose of industry *is* co-operation for public service. The Christian conception of anything is always the real essence of that thing. This is a truth that Christian sociologists often overlook. If Christ were only a moral teacher, then it might be true that what he said was too utopian to be true. But if he also discloses the mind of the Creator of the world, then his thought of anything is what that thing really is. Christ's conception of human nature demands co-operation for its true fulfilment. To be 'realists' we should treat men and women after the example of Christ, as members one of another. If those engaged in industry treat it as if it were an end in itself or as primarily for private profit, or personal gain, then they are treating it as if it were what it is not. God made man that he might use the world and its resources not for his own ends or profit, but that he and his fellows might live a full human life in fellowship with one another. The use of bread and wine in the Eucharist and the fellowship proclaimed at the Communion, suggest that all economic activity should become the instrument and channel of Divine Grace, of that love of God to man the fruit of which is the creation of a human fellowship. The frequent breakdowns in the economic life of the country and the existence of so much wealth while millions die of hunger is the measure of the failure of society to conduct its affairs according to God's will as expressed in every Eucharist.

But such fellowship is dependent on the free co-operation of men and women and this means that we must recognise the value of the individual. Yet our society is such that there are innumerable cases in which it is impressed upon people that they are useless members of the community. It is impossible for them to live sacramental lives, using material things or their natural faculties in the service of their fellow men, or in the development of their own personality. The deepest ground for the challenge of Christianity to much in modern society is that it often outrages the personality of men and women.

If man is in reality one whom God has made, whom he has made in love; if man is one to whom God speaks; if he is the object of Divine solicitude so great that the Word became flesh for his salvation, the Son of God died for him and gives himself to each one individually in Holy Communion — if this be true, then he cannot rightly be treated as a cog in a machine, or a sample of racial bloodstream, or one of the individual atoms that make up a nation. There is no other basis on which the worth of the individual can be maintained. Disinterested love may attain to very great heights on behalf of individuals and groups. But in practice this sacrifical love is extended to only a few persons and in so far as it is given to a community it is nearly always a limited love and therefore compatible with antagonism to other people or communities. There are all around us 'lovers of mankind' who forget the claims of the individual in their devotion to the group. The individual can preserve his value as a person only in so far as he believes that he is greater than human relations will allow. It is significant that alone among the creatures man is a worshipper, seeking fulfilment in that which transcends his finitude. The Christian worship of God as Blessed Trinity affords the ultimate ground for the assurance that the interests of personality and society are not radically opposed; and that only in the unification of his personal and social aims does man reveal his full potentiality.

At the heart of the Eucharist is the Cross and this brings us to a quality of human nature that we scarcely dare apply to social questions, so unpopular it is; this is the need and power of sacrifice. Real progress can only come by self-discipline and sacrifice. This is something that is revealed to us in the Cross and the Eucharist. In a society that had never been corrupted, fellowship might have rested on justice; but once corruption had set in and is in danger of permeating the whole of society, it can only be achieved by sacrifice. The voluntary sacrifice of money, comfort, privilege and pleasure for the sake of others is the healing balm for the wounds of society. When nations are ready to suffer rather than risk the sin of aggression, when Trade Unionists and Employers are ready to suffer rather than damage the welfare of innocent people, when we are all ready to suffer rather than risk the wickedness of consuming more than we contribute, of getting more out of life than we put in for the benefit of our fellows — then and not until then, will men have any rest from the troubles that afflict society.

But this implies a radical change in human nature. Something much more fundamental is required than exhortation. It is the blindness of sin which tends to make a man blind to the contradictions within him, the contradiction between his social nature and his anti-social behaviour. Sin makes men regard their own lives and their existence as the standard by which they judge other men and all other things, without knowing their self-centredness. That is why salvation means that an act of violence must be done to the actual existence of man; it involves the Cross. The salvation which was achieved by the sacrifice of Christ offers to sinful man a means of repentence, a complete turn-about of the human being, so that he is directed towards God and away from himself. *Christian* worship is the act of a man who knows his need of salvation — not improvement, not merely more education — but salvation in the sense of a real reversal or revolution in his attitude to life and God. Worship is the act which disinfects a man from egoism; it lifts the soul out of pre-occupation with itself and its activities, and centres its life upon God.

It would destroy the very nature of worship if we attempted to use worship directly to teach men about the nature of society. S. Augustine said that the essence of evil was to *use* the things we ought to enjoy and to enjoy the things we ought to use. The things we value for what they lead onto — those we use — are different from the things we value for their own sake — those we enjoy. He went on to say that the things to be enjoyed above all else are God the Father, the Son and the Holy Spirit. In worship we value God for his own sake, and Christian worship is only that kind if it is truly objective, bringing the whole of life before God, who is its source. If we have at the back of our minds that it may have some useful purpose, it will not heal men.   That is one of its *effects* and will only happen if it is not regarded as one of its uses. In other words, we must not directly teach *by* worship; we must teach *about* worship and the social implications of worship, hence the title of this chapter. Worship will create an *attitude* to life in which it will be seen that all work and recreation, all art, science and industry, all political and economic life are ways in which we can worship God. The whole direction of life is ideally an act of worship, but of necessity one can be conscious of this only at certain times. It is necessary therefore that certain periods of our life should be set aside which will be consciously devoted to the deliberate act of worshipping God — not as an escape from the responsibilities and problems of life, but primarily to call to mind the fact that we and the whole world stand at every moment in the Presence of God, depend on him for our creation and redemption, and to offer to him for sanctification the whole of life.

It is during those special occasions when we participate in characteristic acts of Christian worship that God's grace is given to us to meet our needs, not as aloof from our daily concerns but as participating in them. It is thus that the worshipper is empowered to live worshipfully. The contrast between the vision seen in the act of worship and the world as it actually is is appalling. The claims of God upon us may seem to be too great, and that nothing can bridge the gulf between the world as we know it and as God would have it. Nor can any human endeavour alone accomplish this. It can be done only through the grace and strength which God imparts. And since grace is a matter of personal relations, it is no arbitrary requirement, but a genuine necessity, that we should enter into the Church's fellowship and participate in its corporate and characteristic acts in order to see the vision and to receive the divine power necessary for doing God's will.

Experience teaches us that association with others in an act of worship can be heartening and uplifting. But beyond this lies the assurance that the Church on earth is united in the worship in heaven and that the visible fellowship is but a part of the total fellowship of faithful men and women. No congregation is alone in the fight for the Kingdom of God upon earth, but amidst all the contradictions of this world in lifting up their hearts and minds to God in worship, they come 'unto the city of the living God, the heavenly Jerusalem, and to the innumerable hosts of angels, to the general assembly and the church of the firstborn, who are enrolled in heaven, and to God the judge of all, and to the spirits of just men made perfect' (Heb. 12.23). Christians believers in Christ, alike living and dead, are united in the Body of Christ. The firstborn of the Christian Church may be regarded as the firstborn of the New Humanity preparing the way for all those who, like them, are united with Christ; through them Creation enters on the beginning of its consummation. So, in the Eucharist, men look forward to the fulfilment of God's purposes when 'earthly bread and new wine . . . elements of the first creation become pledges and first fruits of the new heaven and the new earth' (*Agreed Statement on the Eucharist*, par. 11, by the Anglican-Roman Catholic Commission).

Definite acts of worship thus unite the members of the Church, stimulate their corporate consciousness, widen their vision, and by these experiences enliven their awareness of the Church's opposition to the world when it is organized for godless ends and preserve their sense of the Church's evangelistic task. Though the action of the worshippers is towards God, the fact that they are worshipping is a proclamation to the world. The Church is a worshipping community in the midst of a wider community and its worship has meaning for all the world. All the dim, unspoken yearnings of the human race, find expression in the Church's conscious prayer and glorious praise. And at this point the mind of man is raised from the confused contradictions to the Holy Vision which is the end of all human striving, the real object of all human labour, and the desire of every human heart.

1   'The most effective thing the Church can do, and the most effective thing any individual Christian can do, is to lift up his heart in adoration to God' (William Temple). Do you agree with this?

2   Discuss the different ways in which modern society outrages the personality of men and women.

3   What features in modern society destroy the idea of fellowship expressed in Holy Communion?

4   Is the Resurrection sufficiently emphasized in the liturgy?

5   Should worship be regarded as a means of evangelism?

6   "The truth is that both worship and sociology arise out of christian doctrine, out of the teaching of the christian faith as to what man is and his relation to creation and to God." Do you agree?